Robots

By Elizabeth Tyndall

CELEBRATION PRESS

Pearson Learning Group

Contents

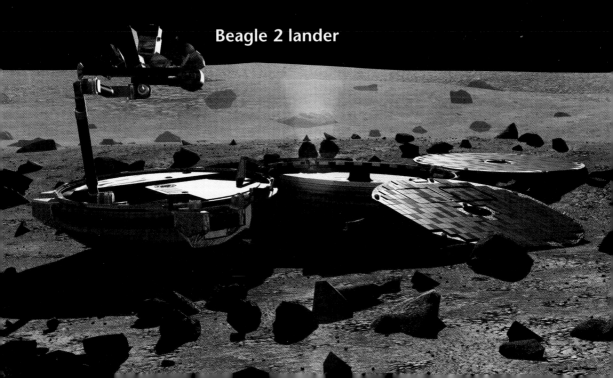

Beagle 2 lander

Robots Around Us

You have probably played with robot toys and have seen robots on television or in movies. These robots probably looked like people. Most real robots, however, do not look like humans at all. You may have seen one and didn't even know it. Robots are found in many places, such as in factories and hospitals and on farms.

Robots are machines that make life easier for people. They help us by doing tasks that are tiring or dangerous. In this book, you can read about the many things robots can do.

toy robots

Robots Are Unique

Robots are different from other machines. Most machines need a person to operate them, but a robot can perform a task **automatically**. A person programs a robot to do a task on its own.

These robots are being programmed.

This is Hobo, a robot that can fight fires and work in dangerous places.

Each robot has a computer called a **controller** for a "brain." A person programs the computer's controller with a set of instructions. The instructions tell the robot exactly what to do.

Wires connect the controller to the robot's **motors**. The controller sends electrical signals to the motors through the wires. Then the motors make the robot or certain of its parts move.

A Robot Motor Controller

controller

wire

wheel

motor

Remote Control
Robots can perform tasks by **remote control**. A person gives the machine instructions from a faraway location. Many machines in space are **telerobotic**, such as the Canadarm2. It receives instructions from scientists to release and repair satellites.

What Powers Robots

Just like other machines, robots need energy to move. Energy comes from a power source. Batteries and solar cells provide one form of power. The electricity found by plugging an electrical cord into a wall socket provides another kind of power. Scientists first decide what a robot is to do. Then they decide the kind of power to use.

Rechargeable batteries are portable and do not need power cords to work. They allow robots to move freely. However, batteries run out of power more quickly than most other power sources.

This underwater robot, called ABE, explores oceans. It runs on large batteries.

This robot, called Sojourner, runs on solar energy. It was built to explore Mars.

Solar energy, or energy from the Sun, is another power source. Solar power is better for robots used in outer space because solar energy is unlimited. These robots must be careful, though, that their power is not cut off by shade. This can happen when another object, such as a planet or large boulder, blocks the sun's light from reaching the robot.

Electricity supplied by power companies is another power source. A robot uses electricity when its electrical cord is plugged into an outlet. Robots such as these have a steady supply of energy, but they cannot move very far.

Electricity provides the power for the robots in this car assembly plant.

Robots on the Move

Robots have changed over time. One of the major changes is in how they move. At first, robots used tracks and wheels, which only allowed them to move over smooth ground. Now robots can move in many different ways.

When we think of robots, we often think of humanoids, which are machines that look like people. These machines often have two legs. Walking on two legs is difficult for robots because it requires balance. Scientists have found that designing a robot that can balance itself is very hard so they have found other ways to make robots move.

In 1865, a walking robot called Steam Man was introduced as a character in a book.

Rodney Brooks, a scientist, studied how insects and spiders move. He saw that they could move quickly and easily. He then created Genghis, the first robot that moves like an insect. Genghis has six legs like an ant or a cockroach. These kinds of robots have few problems balancing as they have several feet planted on the ground.

Gyrobot
Gyrobot is a wheeled robot that was built to study balance and movement. The robot's computer program works with a device inside the robot to balance the robot as it moves.

Genghis can easily move on different surfaces because of its six insect-like legs.

Asimo

Asimo is a robot that walks using two legs. It can walk forward and backward, turn sideways, go around corners, and go up and down stairs.

Today, there are robots that can walk, shuffle, or gallop, such as Asimo, Troody, and Scout II. Scientists have also copied the ways fish move. They have made robots that move under water. The robot Wanda wriggles through the water like a fish. Other underwater robots move by shooting out jets of water, like a squid.

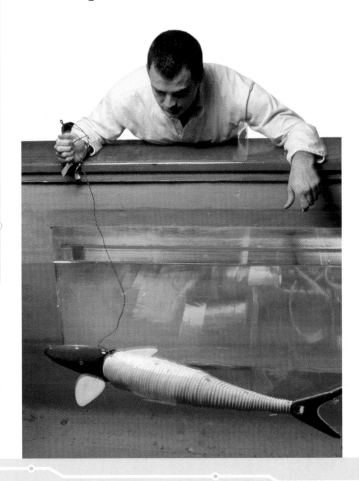

Wanda has flexible skin like a real fish.

Thinking Robots

Scientists are beginning to make robots that can "think" like people. These robots can solve problems. They learn from their mistakes and can adapt to their surroundings. They can even interact with the world around them. To do all of these things, robots must have **sensors**.

The Deep Junior computer and World Chess Champion Gary Kasparov competed against each other in 2003.

Elma

Elma is a six-legged robot that can decide where to walk. Sensors in the robot's legs and head help it walk without running into things. Its controller allows it to learn from its mistakes. However, Elma forgets everything when it is turned off.

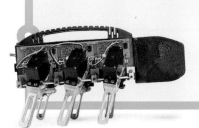

PaPeRo robots use their sensors to move around a room and to communicate with people.

Sensors in a robot are like a person's five senses. Sensors gather information about the robot's environment. They help robots "see" light and "hear" sound. Pressure sensors let robots tell whether objects are hard or soft. Built-in thermometers help them sense heat and cold.

All these sensors let robots make "maps" of the space around them. Then the robots can decide whether they can follow someone's command. If a person tells a robot to turn right and there is a desk in the way, the robot will ignore the command.

Sensors let robots respond to people. Kismet is a robot head. It can sense when a person is too far away or move back if a person is too close. Kismet can talk and can show surprise, fear, happiness, sadness, and anger.

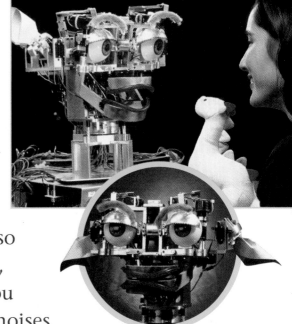

Aibo is a robotic dog that also shows emotions. It uses sounds, body language, and lights. If you pat its head, it makes pleasant noises and lights up. If it is tired, it lowers its head and slows down. Aibo can do more than Kismet. Like a real dog, Aibo can sit, shake hands, fetch a ball, and bark.

Kismet

Working Robots

Robots are especially useful for doing work. [T]can perform jobs that are not safe for people to [do] that people don't want to do over and over aga[in]. These kinds of jobs are ideal for robots.

These women are inspecting food products made by robots.

Robots in Factories

Robots have been used in factories for many years. They help make all kinds of things, from cars to cookies. Robots are very exact. They can do the same thing over and over and do it the same way every time.

This robotic arm can use a white-hot **welder** without getting too hot or tired.

Robotic Hand

A robotic hand can be made of basic machines such as levers and pulleys. A lever is a long bar that moves at one point. A pulley is a wheel over which a cable runs. The levers and cables are moved by motors controlled by a computer.

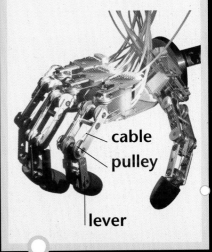

cable

pulley

lever

The robots most often used in factories are **robotic arms**. These arms have motors and cables to make them move. The tool on the end of a robotic arm is called an **effector**. Effectors can be finger-like grippers, drills, saws, or even spray cans.

Robots on Farms

Many different types of farms use robots. Robots can make life much easier for farmers. The milking robot was introduced in the 1990s. It can milk about sixty cows in a day.

a milking robot

Another tool that helps farmers is the intelligent hoe. It can remove weeds growing between rows of crops. A camera on the hoe works with a computer to let the hoe "see" the plants. Scientists are also working on a robot that herds ducks or sheep.

a robot sheepdog

camera

The computer part of the robotic hoe is inside the tractor cab.

Robots in Hospitals

Robots are used in hospitals. They carry supplies to patients and doctors. Some push carts through the hospital making deliveries.

Robots are also used to help perform operations. Robodoc helps out by drilling holes in bones for hip replacements. Robots help train medical students, too. Students can practice performing robot-assisted surgery using a simulator, or training device.

The HelpMate Robot

HelpMate delivers things like meals and medicine. It uses sensors to guide itself through a hospital. HelpMate can be programmed to go to any room and to use elevators.

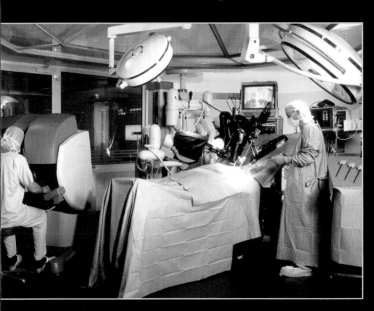

Da Vinci is a robot that helps doctors perform heart surgery.

Robots to the Rescue

Robots can do work that is too dangerous for humans. Some robots work with bomb squads to disconnect bombs safely. If a bomb explodes unexpectedly, the robot may be damaged. However, a robot can be fixed or rebuilt.

Robot helicopters check out accidents when fire or fumes make it too dangerous for a pilot. Robots can also crawl inside nuclear reactors. That's the job of Robug III. It can crawl around unharmed in places where no person would want to go.

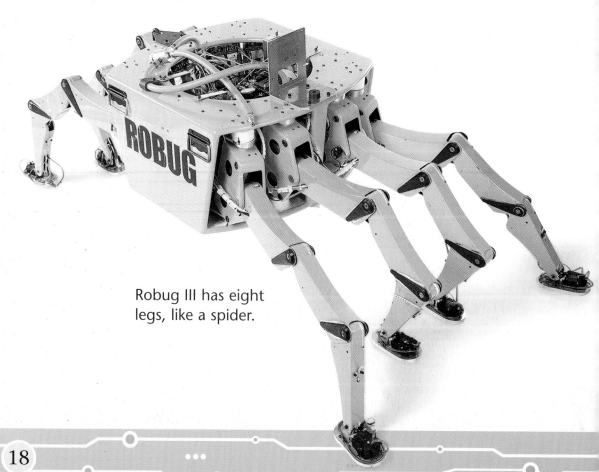

Robug III has eight legs, like a spider.

Robot Explorers

Robots seem to be everywhere—even in outer space. Robots make great space explorers because they don't need oxygen, food, or water. They can travel to planets and locations that are either too far away or too harsh for humans.

In 1999, scientists sent a robot called Stardust to explore a comet. Stardust will try to collect dust from the comet. Scientists hope Stardust will return to Earth with the comet dust in 2006.

Beagle 2
The European Space Agency launched its Mars Express mission on June 2, 2003. Onboard was the robot Beagle 2 lander. This robot is designed to search for signs of life on Mars.

Stardust

Robots are useful under water, too. The water pressure in deep oceans is too great for people. Robots can explore these underwater places much more safely. Some underwater robots, like Jason Jr., are connected by cables to ships or underwater vessels. The crew of the *Alvin* used Jason Jr. to find and explore the wreck of the *Titanic*.

Jason Jr. took photographs of the inside of the *Titanic*.

Other underwater robots, such as Autosub and Seaglider, can move about freely. These robots collect different kinds of data, or information. The data helps scientists to learn about life and conditions under the sea.

▲ Autosub was launched from the RRS *James Clark Ross* to measure ice thickness in Antarctica.

Autosub is powered by more than 4,700 batteries. ▶

Scientists want to learn more about Earth, but some places are almost impossible for people to explore. Robots like Dante II can do these dangerous jobs. In 1994, Dante II investigated an Alaskan volcano. Scientists who were miles away used remote control devices to give it instructions. Dante II climbed the rough land with its eight legs and sent back information.

NASA, the National Aeronautics and Space Administration in the United States, had Dante II built. NASA now knows more about volcanoes. NASA also knows how to make a robot that might walk on the Moon or Mars one day.

Dante II climbed the Mount Spurr volcano to gather information about the inside of the crater.

Future Robots

Today, robots make life easier for many people. Scientists continue to develop new robots for the future. For example, they are working to develop tiny robots that could perform surgery inside a person.

Maybe someday we'll all have robot helpers. We might have robots that walk our dogs, do our shopping, and help with our homework. If you can dream up a robot idea, you can be sure scientists are working on it now.

One day you may be able to watch a robot soccer match with life-size robots.

Glossary

automatically   without direction, on its own

controller   the computer in a robot that is programmed to control its actions

effector   the tool on the end of a robotic arm

motors   devices that use energy to make things move

rechargeable batteries   energy sources that can be renewed by plugging them in to an electrical outlet

remote control   a device that gives instructions to a machine from a distance

robotic arms   robots that remain in one place and that are often used for factory work like painting, drilling, and welding

sensors   parts that get information from the outside world, as our eyes and ears do

telerobotic   the ability of a robot to be controlled by a person from a remote location

welder   a device that applies heat and sometimes filler metal to join two metal parts

Index

the Seven Dwarfs robots